THIS BOOK IS DEDICATED TO THE Stephen G. family,

(Author) Stephen G.

THIS BOOK IS DEDICATED TO THE Stephen G. family, (Author) Stephen G.

Trump Unveiled: The Man, The Presidency, The Impact

Chapter 1: Introduction to Donald J. Trump

Early Life and Background

Donald John Trump was born on June 14, 1946, in Queens, New York City, into a family that would play a significant role in shaping his future. His father, Fred Trump, was a successful real estate developer, and his mother, Mary Anne MacLeod, was a Scottish immigrant. Growing up in a wealthy household, Trump's early life was marked by a sense of privilege, which would later influence his worldview and political aspirations. The family's business acumen and entrepreneurial spirit were instilled in him from a young age, with Fred Trump often involving his children in various real estate ventures. This exposure to the real estate industry would lay the foundation for Donald Trump's later career as a businessman and a politician.

Trump attended the Kew-Forest School in Queens before transferring to the New York Military Academy at the age of 13. The move to a military school was partly due to his parents' concerns about his behavior and academic performance. This environment provided Trump with discipline and leadership skills, which he would later tout as essential qualities during his presidential campaign. After graduating from the military academy, he went on to enroll at Fordham University and later transferred to the Wharton School at the University of Pennsylvania. Graduating with a degree in economics in 1968, Trump's educational background further solidified his interest in business and finance, setting the stage for his future ventures.

Following his graduation, Trump joined his father's real estate business, the Trump Organization, where he initially focused on residential projects in Brooklyn and Queens. However, his ambitions soon led him to Manhattan, where he sought to make a name for himself in a more competitive environment. In the late 1970s, Trump gained significant attention for his bold moves in the New York real estate market, such as the acquisition and renovation of the Commodore Hotel, which became the Grand Hyatt. This project marked the beginning of his rise to prominence and established him as a key player in the city's real estate development scene. His flair for publicity and self-promotion began to emerge during this time, foreshadowing his future as a media personality and political figure.

Trump's ability to leverage media attention was a crucial aspect of his early career. He cultivated a public persona that combined confidence and bravado, often using the media to his advantage. By the 1980s, he was a fixture in tabloids and entertainment news, which helped to further his brand. This relationship with the media would later evolve into a defining characteristic of his presidential campaign and presidency. Trump's ventures expanded beyond real estate into various industries, including casinos and entertainment, solidifying his status as a billionaire businessman. However, he also faced significant setbacks, including bankruptcies that would shape his approach to risk and resilience in the future.

The experiences and challenges of Trump's early life played a pivotal role in molding his political identity. His upbringing in a wealthy family, coupled with his education and early business experiences, fostered a belief in the American Dream and individualism. These themes resonated with many Americans, particularly those who felt disenfranchised by the political establishment. As he transitioned from a businessman to a political figure, Trump's background would serve as a double-edged sword, providing both a base of support and a target for criticism. Understanding Trump's early life and background is essential to grasp the complexities of his presidency and the impact he would have on American politics.

Rise to Prominence in Business

Donald J. Trump's rise to prominence in business is a pivotal chapter in understanding his subsequent political career and the impact he had on American politics. Starting with a modest background, Trump took over his family's real estate business in the 1970s, transforming it into a globally recognized brand. His ambitious vision led to the development of high-profile construction projects, such as Trump Tower in New York City, and a series of successful ventures ranging from casinos to branding deals. This trajectory not only established him as a prominent businessman but also as a household name, which he leveraged effectively during his presidential campaign.

In the 1980s and 1990s, Trump's business dealings were characterized by both significant successes and notable failures. While he achieved considerable wealth and fame, he also faced setbacks, including bankruptcies that affected his casino operations. These challenges, rather than diminishing his status, contributed to a complex narrative that he was able to spin to his advantage. Trump's resilience and ability to rebound from adversity resonated with many Americans, portraying him as a self-made individual who could navigate the complexities of the business world—a narrative that he would later apply to his political identity.

Trump's business acumen extended beyond real estate into various fields, including entertainment and media. His role as the host of "The Apprentice" showcased his personality and business philosophy to millions of viewers, reinforcing his image as a decisive and successful leader. This exposure was instrumental in building his public persona, making him a recognizable figure long before he entered the political arena. His adeptness at using media as a tool for self-promotion laid the groundwork for the unconventional communication strategy he later employed during his presidency.

The interplay between Trump's business dealings and his political aspirations is evident in his economic policies once he assumed office. He advocated for tax cuts, deregulation, and a focus on American manufacturing, all of which were influenced by his experiences in the business world. His administration's economic policies aimed to stimulate growth and create jobs, appealing to his base of supporters who valued his business insights. This alignment of business principles with political strategies was a hallmark of his presidency, reinforcing the narrative of Trump as a businessman-turned-politician.

As Trump rose in prominence, he also faced legal challenges and investigations that scrutinized his business practices. These issues, however, often galvanized his supporters, who viewed them as politically motivated attacks. The loyalty of his base played a crucial role in his resilience against these challenges, highlighting the intersection between his business persona and political identity. Trump's ability to maintain and grow his support amidst controversy showcases how his business rise not only shaped his approach to governance but also influenced American political dynamics in the years that followed.

Entry into Politics

Donald J. Trump's entry into politics marked a significant turning point in American political discourse. Initially known as a businessman and television personality, Trump's transition to a political figure began in earnest when he announced his candidacy for the presidency in June 2015. His campaign was characterized by a populist message that resonated with a significant segment of the American electorate. By positioning himself as an outsider willing to challenge the status quo, Trump tapped into widespread discontent with established political norms, setting the stage for a transformative political movement.

Trump's approach to campaigning was unconventional, utilizing social media platforms extensively to communicate directly with voters. This strategy enabled him to bypass traditional media channels, which he often criticized as biased against him. His use of Twitter became a hallmark of his campaign, allowing him to articulate his views and respond to critics in real-time. This direct engagement not only energized his base but also fundamentally altered the way political communication was conducted, paving the way for future candidates to adopt similar tactics.

The impact of Trump's entry into politics extended beyond his immediate electoral success. His presidency prompted a reevaluation of various political ideologies and party alignments. The Republican Party, in particular, saw a shift as it increasingly embraced Trump's brand of populism, which emphasized nationalism and economic protectionism. This realignment attracted new voters while alienating some traditional conservatives, highlighting the complexities of Trump's influence on American political dynamics.

Trump's policies during his administration reflected his political philosophy and the priorities of his base. His stances on issues such as immigration, economic reform, and foreign relations were often controversial but undeniably impactful. The introduction of the "America First" doctrine reshaped U.S. interactions on the global stage, altering longstanding alliances and trade agreements. These policies sparked intense debates about their long-term implications for American society and the global economy, underscoring the transformative nature of Trump's political approach.

As Trump's presidency faced legal challenges and investigations, his ability to maintain the loyalty of his base became a focal point of his political strategy. This unwavering support allowed him to navigate controversies while continuing to influence the Republican Party and American politics at large. The resilience of his base demonstrated the profound impact he had on shaping modern political landscapes, as his legacy continues to be a subject of analysis and critique within both political and media spheres. The complexities surrounding his entry into politics reveal the intricate interplay between personal branding, policy-making, and the evolving nature of voter engagement in contemporary America.

Chapter 2: The Trump Presidency
Inauguration and First Impressions

The inauguration of Donald J. Trump on January 20, 2017, marked a pivotal moment in American history, not only due to the unconventional nature of his campaign but also because of the stark divisions it revealed within the electorate. As Trump took the oath of office, his speech resonated with themes of nationalism and populism, promising to transfer power from Washington back to the people. This message appealed to his base, which had felt disenfranchised by traditional political elites, while simultaneously raising concerns among many Americans about the implications for democratic norms and institutions.

The immediate aftermath of the inauguration was characterized by a mix of enthusiasm and skepticism. Supporters celebrated the arrival of a leader who they believed would challenge the status quo, while critics voiced apprehensions over Trump's rhetoric and proposed policies. This dichotomy was evident in the media coverage, with networks and publications often taking polarized stances. The portrayal of Trump's presidency began to take shape almost instantly, as commentators analyzed his every move and remark, setting the stage for an administration that would be scrutinized relentlessly.

Trump's approach to economic policy was one of the first areas to attract attention. He promised to revitalize the American economy through tax cuts, deregulation, and a focus on domestic manufacturing. His supporters anticipated an economic renaissance, while skeptics questioned the sustainability of his plans and their potential impact on the national debt. The early days of his presidency saw the administration push forward with initiatives aimed at stimulating growth, yet the complexities of the U.S. economy soon revealed the challenges inherent in achieving those ambitious goals.

Social media became an indispensable tool for Trump, allowing him to communicate directly with his supporters while bypassing traditional media channels. His frequent tweets and unfiltered online presence fueled both his popularity and controversy. This direct engagement not only solidified his base's loyalty but also reshaped the media landscape, prompting discussions about the role of social platforms in politics and the implications for public discourse. Trump's social media strategy would become a defining feature of his presidency, influencing how political communication evolved in the digital age.

As the initial months of Trump's presidency unfolded, his foreign relations strategies also came under scrutiny. His administration's approach was marked by a focus on "America First," leading to a reevaluation of longstanding alliances and trade agreements. Early interactions with global leaders set the tone for a presidency that would challenge diplomatic norms and provoke reactions both domestically and internationally. The evolving nature of these relationships, alongside ongoing legal challenges and investigations, painted a complex portrait of a leader navigating the tumultuous waters of governance. As Trump settled into office, the implications of his inauguration and first impressions were felt far beyond the walls of the White House, shaping the discourse of American politics for years to come.

Key Policies and Initiatives

During his time in office, President Donald J. Trump implemented a range of policies and initiatives that significantly impacted American politics and society. One of the most notable aspects of his presidency was the focus on economic revitalization, which included substantial tax reforms aimed at stimulating growth. The Tax Cuts and Jobs Act of 2017 slashed corporate tax rates and provided individual tax cuts, with the intention of spurring investment and increasing job creation. This policy reflected Trump's broader economic philosophy, which prioritized deregulation and reducing government intervention in the marketplace, setting the stage for significant changes in the U.S. economy.

Trump's approach to foreign relations also marked a departure from traditional diplomatic norms. His administration emphasized "America First," which prioritized national interests in trade agreements and international alliances. This was evident in the renegotiation of NAFTA, resulting in the United States-Mexico-Canada Agreement (USMCA), which aimed to create a more favorable trade environment for American workers. Additionally, Trump's stance towards China included tariffs intended to counteract what he characterized as unfair trade practices, leading to a trade war that redefined U.S.-China relations and had global economic ramifications.

Immigration policy was another cornerstone of Trump's administration, marked by a series of controversial measures aimed at reducing illegal immigration and reforming the legal immigration system. The construction of a border wall along the U.S.-Mexico border became a symbol of his commitment to this cause, alongside efforts to implement stricter immigration enforcement and limit asylum claims. These policies sparked nationwide debates about immigration, national security, and human rights, revealing deep divisions in American society regarding the future of immigration in the United States.

In terms of environmental and energy policies, Trump's administration rolled back numerous regulations aimed at combating climate change and protecting natural resources. The withdrawal from the Paris Agreement highlighted a shift towards prioritizing fossil fuel development and economic growth over environmental considerations. This pivot resonated with many in Trump's base, who viewed energy independence as essential for economic prosperity. However, it also garnered significant criticism from environmental advocates and raised concerns about the long-term implications for climate policy in the U.S.

Throughout his presidency, Trump's relationship with social media played a crucial role in shaping public perception and mobilizing his supporters. He utilized platforms like Twitter to communicate directly with the public, bypassing traditional media channels and creating a unique brand of political engagement. This strategy not only amplified his message but also fostered a sense of community among his supporters, reinforcing their loyalty. However, it also led to significant controversies, particularly regarding the spread of misinformation and the subsequent reactions by social media companies, which raised questions about censorship, free speech, and the role of technology in modern politics. These key policies and initiatives collectively illustrate the complexities of Trump's presidency and his enduring impact on American political discourse.

Major Events Throughout the Presidency

Major events throughout Donald Trump's presidency shaped not only his administration but also the broader political landscape in the United States. His tenure, marked by significant and often controversial decisions, reflected a shift in both domestic and foreign policies that resonated with his supporters and critics alike. From the early days of his presidency, when he enacted sweeping changes to immigration policy, to his handling of the COVID-19 pandemic, each major event revealed the challenges and complexities of his leadership style.

One of the earliest and most impactful actions of Trump's presidency was the implementation of the travel ban, which aimed to restrict entry from several predominantly Muslim countries. This decision ignited fierce debates over national security and civil rights, polarizing public opinion and leading to numerous legal challenges. The travel ban not only highlighted Trump's hardline stance on immigration but also set the tone for his administration's policies, which consistently emphasized a focus on border security and reduced immigration levels.

Trump's economic policies also played a crucial role in shaping his presidency. The Tax Cuts and Jobs Act of 2017, a hallmark of his administration, aimed to stimulate economic growth through significant tax reductions for individuals and corporations. While supporters argued that it spurred job creation and investment, critics contended that it disproportionately benefited the wealthy and increased the federal deficit. The economic landscape during his presidency, including the pre-pandemic growth and the subsequent downturn, illustrated the volatility of his policies and their far-reaching implications for American workers and businesses.

The role of social media became increasingly prominent during Trump's presidency, fundamentally altering the way political discourse unfolded. His frequent use of platforms like Twitter allowed him to communicate directly with his base, bypassing traditional media channels. This unfiltered approach fostered a unique relationship between Trump and his supporters, but it also led to widespread misinformation and heightened political tensions. The impact of social media on public perception and political mobilization during his presidency cannot be overstated, as it reshaped the dynamics of engagement and activism in contemporary politics.

Throughout his time in office, Trump faced multiple legal challenges and investigations, which further defined his presidency. The inquiry into Russian interference in the 2016 election, culminating in the Mueller Report, and the impeachment trials over his dealings with Ukraine were significant events that tested the resilience of American institutions. These controversies not only galvanized his base but also intensified opposition from Democrats and other critics. The legal battles underscored the contentious nature of his presidency, highlighting the deep divisions within American society and the ongoing struggle over the rule of law and accountability in governance.

Chapter 3: Trump's Impact on American Politics

Shifting Political Paradigms

Shifting political paradigms during Donald Trump's presidency marked a significant transformation in the landscape of American politics. This change was characterized by a departure from traditional political norms and the emergence of new dynamics that reshaped party alignments, voter engagement, and policy discourse. The Republican Party, once seen as the bastion of conservatism, found itself increasingly influenced by populist sentiments and a focus on identity politics, largely driven by Trump's rhetoric and his ability to connect with a segment of the electorate that felt marginalized by mainstream political discourse.

One of the most notable shifts was the role of social media in political engagement. Trump's adept use of platforms like Twitter redefined how politicians communicate with the public, bypassing traditional media gatekeepers. His unfiltered messages not only energized his base but also sparked widespread controversy and debate, leading to a new era of political communication. This direct approach fostered a sense of intimacy and immediacy with supporters, allowing for real-time interaction that traditional campaigns had rarely achieved. The implications of this shift extended beyond Trump's presidency, influencing how future candidates approach voter outreach and engagement.

Economically, Trump's administration introduced policies that diverged from conventional Republican strategies. His focus on protectionism, exemplified by tariffs on foreign goods, aimed to bolster American manufacturing and address trade imbalances. This approach resonated with many working-class voters who had felt the repercussions of globalization. However, it also prompted significant debate about the long-term impacts on the economy and international relations. The economic policies during Trump's presidency not only reflected a shift in priorities but also highlighted the changing perceptions of what it means to be a conservative in today's political climate.

Foreign relations under Trump also exemplified a departure from established paradigms. The administration's "America First" approach led to a reassessment of long-standing alliances and international commitments. Key decisions, such as withdrawing from the Paris Climate Agreement and the Iran nuclear deal, illustrated a willingness to prioritize national interests over multilateral cooperation. This strategy garnered both support and criticism, raising questions about the future of U.S. leadership on the global stage and the potential repercussions for international diplomacy.

Lastly, the legal challenges and investigations that surrounded Trump's presidency further underscored the shifting political landscape.

The unprecedented nature of these inquiries into a sitting president highlighted the contentious relationship between the executive branch and the judiciary. As investigations unfolded, they not only affected Trump's political standing but also catalyzed discussions about accountability, the rule of law, and the integrity of democratic institutions. The complexities of these legal battles illustrated how political paradigms can shift dramatically, influencing public perception and shaping the discourse surrounding governance and ethics in America.

The Republican Party Under Trump

The Republican Party underwent a significant transformation during Donald Trump's presidency, which began in January 2017. Trump's rise to power reshaped the party's identity, moving it away from traditional conservatism towards a more populist and nationalist agenda. This shift attracted a diverse coalition of supporters who resonated with Trump's anti-establishment rhetoric and his promise to prioritize American interests. The embrace of Trump's persona and policies indicated a departure from the previous Republican leadership, leading to a redefined base that valued loyalty to Trump over adherence to longstanding party ideologies.

One of the key aspects of Trump's influence on the Republican Party was his approach to economic policies. Under his administration, the party championed tax cuts, deregulation, and a focus on job creation within the manufacturing sector. The Tax Cuts and Jobs Act of 2017 was a landmark achievement that aimed to stimulate growth by reducing corporate tax rates and providing tax relief to individuals. While supporters argued that these measures strengthened the economy, critics pointed to rising deficits and income inequality as significant consequences of this economic strategy. The debate around these policies illustrated a broader ideological shift within the party, prioritizing immediate economic gains over traditional conservative fiscal responsibility.

Social media became a powerful tool for Trump, fundamentally altering the way political communication occurred. His adept use of platforms like Twitter allowed him to bypass traditional media, directly engaging with his supporters and shaping public discourse. This strategy not only bolstered his personal brand but also mobilized his base, creating a sense of community among followers. However, it also led to the spread of misinformation and heightened polarization within the political landscape. The Republican Party, under Trump's influence, increasingly embraced social media as a means of campaigning and rallying support, further entrenching the divide between party loyalists and critics.

Trump's foreign relations strategies marked another significant departure from previous Republican policies. His administration adopted an "America First" approach, emphasizing bilateral agreements over multilateral cooperation and often questioning traditional alliances. The withdrawal from the Paris Agreement on climate change and the renegotiation of trade deals, such as NAFTA, reflected this shift. While some hailed these moves as necessary for protecting American interests, others raised concerns about the long-term implications for global stability and U.S. leadership on the world stage. These policies sparked intense debate within the party about the direction of American foreign policy and the role of the U.S. in international affairs.

Legal challenges and investigations also loomed large over Trump's presidency, affecting the Republican Party's dynamics. From the Mueller investigation into Russian interference in the 2016 election to impeachment proceedings, Trump's legal battles created a constant backdrop of controversy. While many in the party rallied around Trump, viewing these challenges as politically motivated attacks, others expressed unease about the implications for the party's future. The response to these issues highlighted a growing divide within the Republican Party, as some members sought to distance themselves from Trump while others remained steadfast in their support. This conflict raised critical questions about the party's direction and the lasting impact of Trump's presidency on American politics.

Polarization and Partisanship

Polarization and partisanship have become defining features of American politics in recent years, with President Donald J. Trump often seen as both a catalyst and a product of these trends. The stark divisions within the electorate have deepened, affecting not only how political parties operate but also how citizens engage with one another on a social level. This polarization is evident in the extreme loyalty displayed by party members, particularly among Trump's base, who have rallied around his policies and persona with fervor. This loyalty often translates into a willingness to overlook controversies and embrace a narrative that is heavily influenced by partisan media.

The rise of social media has played a significant role in exacerbating these divisions. Platforms such as Twitter and Facebook have allowed for the rapid dissemination of information, but they have also facilitated the spread of misinformation and extreme viewpoints. Trump's adept use of social media to communicate directly with supporters has bypassed traditional media filters, fostering a sense of connection and urgency among his base. However, this same dynamic has led to an environment where facts are often secondary to beliefs, contributing to a landscape where partisan narratives dominate discourse.

Trump's economic policies also reflect and reinforce partisan divides. Supporters argue that his administration's tax cuts and deregulation efforts spurred economic growth and job creation, while critics contend that these measures disproportionately benefited the wealthy and increased income inequality. This divergence in interpretation illustrates how economic issues are increasingly viewed through a partisan lens, with individuals often aligning their opinions with their political identity rather than an objective analysis of the data. As a result, economic discussions that should ideally be grounded in common interests are frequently polarized along party lines.

Foreign relations under Trump further exemplify the impact of partisanship. His administration's approach to international alliances and trade agreements has been met with both staunch support and fierce opposition, reflecting the broader ideological divides within American society. Trump's skepticism of multilateral agreements and his emphasis on "America First" policies have resonated with many of his supporters, who perceive these actions as a necessary shift away from what they view as ineffective globalism. Conversely, critics argue that this approach undermines America's standing in the world and emboldens adversaries, showcasing how foreign policy has become another battleground for partisan conflict.

Ultimately, the polarization and partisanship that have intensified during Trump's presidency pose significant challenges for American democracy. As citizens become more entrenched in their views, the potential for constructive dialogue diminishes, leading to the erosion of social cohesion. The implications of this divide extend beyond politics, affecting community relationships and fostering an environment where compromise becomes increasingly difficult. Understanding these dynamics is crucial for anyone looking to grasp the full impact of Trump's presidency on American life and the future trajectory of the nation.

Chapter 4: Economic Policies Under Trump's Administration

Tax Reform

Tax reform was a cornerstone of President Donald J. Trump's economic agenda, reflecting his administration's commitment to stimulating growth and altering the landscape of American fiscal policy. The Tax Cuts and Jobs Act of 2017, the most significant overhaul of the U.S. tax code in over three decades, aimed to reduce the corporate tax rate from 35% to 21%, incentivizing domestic investment and job creation. By lowering individual tax rates and nearly doubling the standard deduction, the legislation sought to provide immediate relief to middle-class families while also simplifying the tax filing process. The administration argued that these changes would lead to more money in Americans' pockets, fostering consumer spending and economic expansion.

While proponents of the tax reform celebrated its potential to invigorate the economy, critics raised concerns about its long-term implications for income inequality and federal deficit levels. The reform disproportionately benefited corporations and wealthier individuals, leading some analysts to argue that it could exacerbate economic divides. Additionally, the decision to eliminate certain deductions, such as the state and local tax (SALT) deduction, disproportionately affected taxpayers in high-tax states, sparking intense debate and calls for revisions. This division illustrated the broader ideological rift in American politics regarding taxation and government spending, as Democrats criticized the reform as a giveaway to the wealthy.

The impact of Trump's tax reform on the economy was a subject of extensive analysis and debate. Supporters pointed to robust GDP growth and a historically low unemployment rate during the early years of his presidency as evidence of the policy's success. The administration emphasized that the tax cuts led to significant corporate investment and wage increases, showcasing examples of companies giving bonuses to employees as a direct result of the reform. However, detractors pointed out that the benefits were not uniformly experienced across all sectors of society, with many working-class Americans feeling little tangible improvement in their financial situation.

Social media played a crucial role in shaping public perception of the tax reform. The Trump administration effectively utilized platforms like Twitter to communicate its message, rallying support and countering criticisms in real-time. This direct line of communication allowed Trump to present his tax policies in a favorable light, often framing them as a success story of his presidency. However, the rapid dissemination of information also facilitated the spread of misinformation and polarized views, as opponents used social media to highlight the potential downsides of the reform, such as increased deficits and cuts to essential services.

Ultimately, the legacy of Trump's tax reform will be assessed not only by its immediate economic outcomes but also by its long-term effects on American fiscal policy and societal equity. The debate surrounding the reform reflects broader themes of governance and economic philosophy that continue to resonate in contemporary American politics. As the nation grapples with the implications of Trump's presidency, the discussions sparked by his tax policies will likely influence future legislative efforts and the overall direction of the American economy.

Trade Policies and Tariffs

Trade policies and tariffs form a crucial component of President Donald J. Trump's economic strategy, significantly impacting both domestic and international markets. Upon taking office in January 2017, Trump made it clear that he intended to prioritize American industry and workers. His administration's approach leaned heavily on revising existing trade agreements and imposing tariffs on imports, particularly from countries he deemed unfair trading partners, such as China. This shift was encapsulated in Trump's "America First" agenda, which sought to reduce trade deficits and encourage domestic manufacturing while simultaneously reshaping America's role in the global economy.

One of the most notable actions taken by the Trump administration was the imposition of tariffs on steel and aluminum imports. In March 2018, Trump announced tariffs of 25 percent on steel and 10 percent on aluminum, citing national security concerns as a justification under Section 232 of the Trade Expansion Act of 1962. This move was aimed at protecting American steel and aluminum producers from foreign competition and was met with both support and criticism. Supporters argued that these tariffs would revive struggling industries and create jobs, while critics warned of potential retaliatory measures from affected countries, which could lead to a trade war.

The administration's trade policies culminated in a renegotiation of the North American Free Trade Agreement (NAFTA), resulting in the United States-Mexico-Canada Agreement (USMCA). This agreement aimed to modernize trade relations between the three countries, addressing issues such as labor rights, environmental protections, and digital trade. While the USMCA was celebrated as a win for American workers, its long-term effectiveness remains a topic of debate among economists and policymakers. The complexities of trade relationships in an interconnected global economy pose challenges that may not be fully addressed by such agreements.

Trump's trade policies also extended to China, where the administration launched a series of tariffs on Chinese goods, leading to a trade conflict that reverberated through global markets. The tariffs were intended to combat intellectual property theft and unfair trade practices, but they also sparked significant economic repercussions, including increased prices for American consumers and strains on global supply chains. This approach reflected a broader shift in U.S. foreign policy, emphasizing a more confrontational stance toward China and signaling a growing recognition of the geopolitical implications of trade.

The impact of Trump's trade policies and tariffs on American politics and the economy continues to be analyzed and debated. While his base largely supported these measures as necessary for protecting American jobs and industries, the broader implications for international relations and economic stability remain complex. As the United States navigates its post-Trump era, the legacy of these trade policies will likely influence future administrations and the ongoing discourse surrounding American economic strategy and global engagement.

Job Growth and Unemployment Rates

Job growth and unemployment rates are critical indicators of economic health and are often closely monitored during any presidential administration. Under President Donald J. Trump, there was a notable emphasis on job creation and reducing unemployment, which became a cornerstone of his economic policies. Trump's administration implemented tax cuts and deregulation initiatives aimed at stimulating business growth and encouraging companies to hire more workers. These strategies appealed to many Americans, particularly those in the manufacturing and energy sectors, who felt the impacts of globalization and economic shifts in the preceding years.

In the early years of Trump's presidency, the U.S. experienced a significant drop in unemployment rates, reaching historic lows by 2019. The administration touted these statistics as evidence of the success of its economic policies. Job growth was particularly evident in sectors like construction, manufacturing, and healthcare. Many supporters viewed these developments as a vindication of Trump's approach, believing that his focus on American jobs and nationalism shifted the economic landscape positively. This period was characterized by a robust stock market and rising consumer confidence, which were often highlighted in Trump's communications, particularly through social media platforms.

However, the COVID-19 pandemic in 2020 dramatically altered the economic trajectory and brought unprecedented challenges. The sudden shutdown of businesses and stay-at-home orders led to a sharp spike in unemployment rates, reaching levels not seen since the Great Depression. This crisis underscored the fragility of the job market and raised questions about the sustainability of the economic gains achieved prior to the pandemic. The Trump administration's response included stimulus packages and efforts to reopen the economy, but the recovery was uneven and highlighted disparities in job loss across different demographics and industries.

As the pandemic unfolded, discussions about job growth and unemployment also became intertwined with broader social and economic issues, such as racial inequality and access to employment opportunities. The Black Lives Matter movement, along with other social movements, drew attention to systemic issues that affected job prospects for marginalized communities. Trump's administration faced criticism for its handling of these concerns, which some felt were sidelined in favor of a focus on overall economic metrics. This period also saw a rise in debates about the future of work, with remote work becoming more prevalent and reshaping the labor market.

In evaluating Trump's impact on job growth and unemployment rates, it becomes clear that while significant gains were made during the early years of his presidency, the pandemic introduced complications that challenged the narrative of success. The long-term effects of his policies and their implications for future job creation remain subjects of ongoing analysis and debate. As the country moves forward, understanding the interplay between economic policies, job growth, and the evolving workforce will be essential in shaping the future of American labor and the broader economy.

Chapter 5: Trump and Social Media Influence

The Role of Twitter in Communication

Twitter has transformed the landscape of communication, particularly in the realm of politics, where it has become a pivotal platform for leaders to engage with the public directly. For President Donald J. Trump, Twitter served not only as a communication tool but also as a means to shape his narrative and bypass traditional media filters. In an era where information travels at lightning speed, Trump's use of Twitter allowed him to disseminate his thoughts, policies, and reactions instantaneously, creating a direct line to his supporters and detractors alike.

The immediacy of Twitter enabled Trump to respond to events in real time, often using the platform to announce policy decisions or to comment on ongoing political issues. His tweets often sparked national conversations, drawing media attention and public discourse. This ability to set the agenda and dominate headlines was particularly significant during his presidency, as he frequently used Twitter to frame issues according to his perspective, influencing how they were perceived by the public and the media. In this way, Trump utilized Twitter not just as a means of communication, but as a strategic tool in his political arsenal.

Moreover, Twitter helped solidify Trump's connection with his base, fostering a sense of community among his supporters. By sharing personal anecdotes, retweeting supporters, and engaging with followers, Trump cultivated an interactive environment that resonated with many Americans. This direct engagement allowed him to reinforce his policies on immigration, economic strategies, and foreign relations while simultaneously rallying support against perceived opposition. The platform became an echo chamber where his supporters felt seen and heard, enhancing their loyalty and commitment to his presidency.

However, Trump's Twitter presence also attracted significant criticism and scrutiny. His use of the platform was often controversial, leading to polarized opinions and sometimes inciting backlash. Critics argued that his tweets frequently undermined diplomatic relations and contributed to a divisive political climate. Moreover, the rapid spread of misinformation through social media raised concerns about the implications for public discourse and democratic processes. Despite these challenges, Trump's ability to leverage Twitter for communication underscored its growing importance in modern politics.

In conclusion, Twitter played a crucial role in President Trump's communication strategy, offering both opportunities and challenges. The platform allowed him to engage directly with the electorate, shape public discourse, and reinforce his political identity. As Trump's presidency unfolded, the influence of Twitter highlighted not only the potential for social media to alter political communication but also the complexities that arise when a leader harnesses such powerful tools. The legacy of Trump's use of Twitter continues to provoke discussions about the future of political engagement in an increasingly digital world.

Social Media Strategies and Campaigns

Social media has transformed the landscape of political communication, and President Donald J. Trump's use of these platforms has been particularly notable. His strategies and campaigns on social media not only helped him secure the presidency in 2016 but also shaped the way political discourse is conducted in the United States. Trump's approach involved a combination of direct engagement with supporters, a willingness to bypass traditional media, and a focus on viral content that resonated with his base. This chapter delves into the specific strategies employed by Trump, highlighting how they contributed to his political brand and legacy.

One of the most significant aspects of Trump's social media strategy was his ability to connect directly with voters. By utilizing platforms such as Twitter and Facebook, he effectively engaged his audience without the filter of traditional media outlets. This direct communication allowed him to share his thoughts, rally support, and respond to criticism in real-time. His tweets often served as rallying cries for his followers, reinforcing his messages and fostering a sense of community among his supporters. This approach not only energized his base but also demonstrated the potential of social media as a tool for political mobilization.

Trump's campaigns on social media also capitalized on the creation of shareable content that appealed to the emotions and values of his supporters. Memes, videos, and graphics that depicted his policies and character in a favorable light circulated widely, often going viral and reaching audiences far beyond his direct followers. The use of provocative language and imagery also played a crucial role in capturing attention and driving engagement. By crafting messages that were both relatable and controversial, Trump maintained a constant presence in public discourse, ensuring that his agenda remained at the forefront of political conversations.

Another key element of Trump's social media strategy was his adeptness at utilizing data analytics to target specific demographics. His campaigns harnessed sophisticated tools to identify and engage potential voters based on their interests and online behavior. This data-driven approach allowed Trump's team to tailor their messaging to resonate with various segments of the electorate, enhancing the effectiveness of their campaigns. By understanding the preferences and concerns of different voter groups, Trump was able to focus his efforts on swing states and demographics that were crucial to his electoral success.

The impact of Trump's social media presence extends beyond his campaigns; it has fundamentally altered the dynamics of American politics. His unconventional use of these platforms has encouraged other politicians to adopt similar strategies, resulting in a more fragmented and polarized political environment. Moreover, the normalization of direct engagement through social media has led to a shift in how political narratives are constructed and disseminated. As Trump's influence persists, understanding his social media strategies offers valuable insights into the evolving nature of political communication and the role of technology in shaping public opinion.

Impact on Public Perception

The impact of Donald Trump's presidency on public perception has been profound and multifaceted, reshaping the political landscape in ways that continue to resonate today. One of the most notable aspects of this shift has been the polarization of American society. Trump's tenure saw an increase in divisions among the electorate, with supporters and opponents often entrenched in their views. This polarization has affected not only political discourse but also social interactions, as individuals increasingly align themselves with groups that reflect their beliefs, further entrenching the divide.

Media coverage of Trump has played a critical role in shaping public perception. The 24-hour news cycle, combined with the rise of social media platforms, created an environment where Trump's actions and statements were amplified and scrutinized like never before. This relentless coverage often focused on controversy, leading to a perception of Trump as a divisive figure. While his supporters praised him for challenging the status quo, critics viewed his rhetoric and policies as harmful. The dichotomy in media portrayals contributed to a fragmented public perception, with individuals gravitating toward narratives that reinforced their existing beliefs.

Trump's economic policies also influenced public perception, particularly regarding issues like job creation and tax reform. Supporters credited him with fostering economic growth and lowering unemployment rates prior to the COVID-19 pandemic, which bolstered his image as a successful businessman turned politician. However, critics pointed to rising income inequality and concerns over long-term economic sustainability. This discrepancy in interpretation highlighted the complexities of economic performance and its perception, as different demographics experienced varying impacts from his policies.

The role of social media in Trump's presidency cannot be understated. His adept use of platforms like Twitter allowed him to communicate directly with his base and bypass traditional media filters, shaping narratives on his terms. This direct engagement fostered a sense of community among supporters, reinforcing loyalty and creating a feedback loop that influenced public perception. However, it also raised concerns about misinformation and the spread of divisive rhetoric, as critics argued that social media amplified extremist views and contributed to societal tensions.

Finally, Trump's foreign relations strategies contributed to a mixed public perception. His unconventional approach, characterized by both confrontation and negotiation, drew both praise and criticism. Supporters applauded his efforts to engage with North Korea and challenge longstanding alliances, viewing these actions as bold and necessary. In contrast, detractors expressed concern over the potential destabilization of international relationships and the implications for global security. This dichotomy in public perception underscores the complex legacy of Trump's presidency, as differing viewpoints continue to shape discussions about his impact on American politics and society.

Chapter 6: Trump's Foreign Relations Strategies

Relations with NATO and Allies

President Donald J. Trump's approach to NATO and relations with traditional allies marked a significant departure from previous administrations. Throughout his presidency, Trump consistently emphasized the need for NATO member countries to increase their defense spending. He argued that many nations were not meeting the alliance's guideline of spending at least two percent of their GDP on defense, which he believed placed an unfair burden on the United States. This stance was met with both support and criticism; while some applauded his call for greater burden-sharing, others feared it could weaken the alliance's cohesion and collective security.

Trump's rhetoric often included sharp critiques of specific allies, notably Germany, for its reliance on Russian energy imports while failing to contribute adequately to NATO's funding. These comments stirred tensions within the alliance and raised questions about the future of U.S. commitment to NATO. Nevertheless, Trump's administration sought to reassure allies of America's commitment through increased military presence in Eastern Europe and participation in NATO exercises, aiming to counteract Russian aggression while simultaneously pushing for reforms within the alliance.

The Trump administration also navigated complex relationships with non-NATO allies. His foreign policy approach was characterized by a preference for bilateral agreements over multilateral ones. This strategy led to a reevaluation of partnerships, as seen in the U.S.-Japan trade negotiations and the efforts to strengthen ties with countries in the Indo-Pacific region. Trump's focus on economic interests and trade imbalances often overshadowed traditional diplomatic practices, leading to an unpredictable but impactful foreign policy landscape.

Social media played a pivotal role in shaping Trump's foreign relations strategies, allowing him to communicate directly with both domestic and international audiences. His tweets often set the tone for diplomatic relations, sometimes creating confusion or backlash among allies. The use of platforms such as Twitter enabled Trump to bypass traditional media filters, yet it also raised concerns about the implications of such direct communication on international diplomacy and the stability of long-standing alliances.

Despite the controversies surrounding his approach, Trump's presidency left a lasting impact on NATO and U.S. relations with allies. His tenure prompted a re-examination of the alliance's strategic priorities and defense spending commitments. While some allies expressed concern over the unpredictability of U.S. foreign policy under Trump, others recognized his influence in initiating discussions about defense spending and burden-sharing that continue to shape NATO's agenda today. Trump's legacy in this area remains a topic of debate, reflecting the complex interplay between national interests, international cooperation, and the evolving nature of global alliances.

Engagement with North Korea

Engagement with North Korea during Donald Trump's presidency marked a significant departure from previous administrations' approaches to the isolated nation. Trump's strategy was characterized by a blend of unconventional diplomacy and bombastic rhetoric. Unlike his predecessors, who largely focused on sanctions and diplomatic isolation, Trump sought direct engagement with North Korean leader Kim Jong-un. This shift was not without controversy, as it raised questions about the efficacy of dialogue with a regime known for its nuclear ambitions and human rights violations. Trump's willingness to engage directly with Kim was emblematic of his broader foreign policy ethos, which prioritized personal diplomacy over established diplomatic protocols.

The high-profile summits between Trump and Kim in 2018 and 2019 were unprecedented in the context of U.S.-North Korea relations. The first summit, held in Singapore, was particularly notable for the symbolic gestures exchanged, including Trump's decision to suspend military exercises with South Korea. This move was aimed at fostering a more conducive environment for negotiations but was met with criticism from defense experts and political opponents who argued it undermined regional security. The subsequent summit in Hanoi, however, ended without a concrete agreement, highlighting the challenges inherent in negotiating with a regime that has historically employed brinkmanship as a negotiating tactic.

Trump's engagement strategy was also significantly influenced by his understanding of social media's role in shaping public perception and foreign policy narratives. By using platforms like Twitter to announce his meetings with Kim and to address issues related to North Korea, Trump sought to control the narrative and rally support among his base. This approach underscored his belief that direct communication, both with the public and foreign leaders, could lead to tangible outcomes. However, the reliance on social media also meant that any diplomatic missteps were amplified in real time, contributing to a volatile diplomatic environment.

The economic implications of Trump's North Korea policy were equally notable. His administration maintained a firm stance on sanctions while simultaneously engaging in dialogue. Trump often touted his personal rapport with Kim as a potential pathway to denuclearization and economic cooperation. The idea was that improved relations could lead to economic benefits for both nations, particularly for North Korea, which has long struggled under international sanctions. Critics argued that the emphasis on personal chemistry overshadowed the complexities of dismantling North Korea's nuclear program and that Trump's approach risked legitimizing a regime that had little intention of relinquishing its nuclear arsenal.

Ultimately, Trump's engagement with North Korea left a complex legacy. While the summits themselves were historic, the lack of substantive progress on denuclearization and continued missile tests by North Korea raised questions about the long-term effectiveness of this approach. The interplay of Trump's unique diplomatic style, the influence of social media, and the geopolitical realities of the Korean Peninsula created a multifaceted situation that continues to shape discussions about U.S. foreign policy. As historians and analysts evaluate Trump's impact on American politics, the engagement with North Korea will undoubtedly be a focal point, illustrating the challenges and unpredictability of modern diplomacy.

Trade Relations with China

Trade relations with China have been a focal point of President Donald J. Trump's administration, reflecting a broader strategy aimed at reshaping America's economic landscape. Upon taking office, Trump identified the trade deficit with China as a significant issue, alleging that unfair trade practices were harming American workers. His administration launched a series of initiatives aimed at renegotiating trade agreements and imposing tariffs on a variety of Chinese goods. This approach marked a departure from previous administrations, which had often favored engagement and cooperation over confrontation in trade matters.

One of the hallmark strategies of Trump's trade policy was the implementation of tariffs, which were seen as a tool to protect American manufacturing and address perceived imbalances in trade. The administration imposed tariffs on billions of dollars' worth of Chinese imports, claiming that these measures would incentivize domestic production and reduce dependency on foreign goods. Critics argued that such tariffs could lead to retaliatory measures from China, potentially escalating into a broader trade war. Nonetheless, Trump maintained that these actions were essential for leveling the playing field and securing fairer terms for American businesses.

The trade negotiations between the United States and China were marked by high-stakes discussions and a series of ups and downs. The administration engaged in extensive dialogue over several years, which culminated in the signing of the Phase One trade agreement in January 2020. This agreement aimed to address issues such as intellectual property theft, currency manipulation, and increased purchases of American agricultural products by China. While the agreement was hailed by some as a step toward resolving longstanding trade tensions, others viewed it as insufficient in fundamentally altering the trade relationship between the two nations.

Trump's trade policies also had significant implications for global supply chains and international economic relations. The tariffs imposed on Chinese goods prompted many American companies to reevaluate their sourcing strategies, leading some to relocate their manufacturing operations to other countries. This shift highlighted the interconnectedness of global markets and raised questions about the long-term viability of tariffs as a solution to trade imbalances. Trump's approach ignited debates over economic nationalism versus globalization, with his base largely supporting the former as a means of protecting American jobs.

The influence of social media played a crucial role in shaping public perception of trade relations with China during Trump's presidency. Trump frequently utilized platforms like Twitter to communicate his views on trade, framing the narrative around American interests and the need for a tougher stance against China. His direct engagement with supporters through social media helped solidify his base's approval of his trade policies, contributing to a broader discourse on American economic sovereignty. As the administration navigated complex trade dynamics, the intertwining of social media and trade policy underscored the evolving nature of political communication in the digital age.

Chapter 7: Trump's Legal Challenges and Investigations

Overview of Major Investigations

Impeachment Proceedings

Impeachment proceedings against President Donald J. Trump marked a significant chapter in American political history, revealing deep divisions within the government and the electorate. The first impeachment, initiated in December 2019, stemmed from allegations that Trump solicited foreign interference in the 2020 election by pressing Ukraine to investigate his political rival, Joe Biden. This event not only underscored the contentious nature of contemporary American politics but also showcased the evolving role of the presidency in relation to congressional oversight and accountability.

As the impeachment inquiry unfolded, it became evident that the process would be heavily influenced by party lines. House Democrats, motivated by a commitment to uphold constitutional norms, pushed for impeachment, while Republicans largely rallied around Trump, framing the inquiry as a partisan attack. The proceedings were marked by intense media coverage, with various outlets providing differing narratives that reflected their political biases. This polarization in media reporting further entrenched the divide among the American public, highlighting how Trump's presidency had transformed media dynamics and public discourse.

The Senate trial, which began in January 2020, was characterized by procedural debates and the absence of witness testimonies, a decision that drew criticism from Democrats and some independent observers. Ultimately, Trump was acquitted by the Senate, with most Republican senators voting to dismiss the charges. This outcome illustrated the loyalty Trump commanded within his party and reaffirmed the strong influence of his base, which remained steadfast in its support despite the gravity of the impeachment charges. The acquittal set a precedent for future presidential conduct and raised questions about the effectiveness of impeachment as a tool for political accountability.

Trump's second impeachment in January 2021 followed the Capitol riot on January 6, where he was accused of inciting an insurrection against the government. This unprecedented event not only led to swift condemnation from a portion of the political spectrum but also highlighted the complexities of Trump's influence on American politics. The rapid evolution of social media as a platform for political communication played a crucial role in shaping the narrative around the events, as Trump's use of Twitter and other platforms served to mobilize his supporters and spread misinformation.

The legacy of Trump's impeachment proceedings will likely be felt for years to come, influencing how future administrations navigate the balance of power, public accountability, and party loyalty. As discussions surrounding Trump's impact on American politics continue, the impeachment saga serves as a reminder of the fragility of democratic institutions and the ongoing challenges faced in maintaining their integrity. It also raises important questions about the role of the media, the interpretations of justice, and the responsibilities of elected officials to their constituents and the Constitution.

Ongoing Legal Issues Post-Presidency

Ongoing legal issues post-presidency have emerged as a significant aspect of Donald J. Trump's narrative following his time in office. After leaving the White House, Trump has faced a series of investigations and lawsuits that have drawn considerable attention from both the media and the public. These legal challenges span various domains, including business practices, election-related allegations, and personal conduct, creating a complex legal landscape that could have lasting implications for Trump and his political legacy.

One of the most prominent legal issues Trump faces involves the investigations into his business dealings. Authorities are scrutinizing his financial practices, including allegations of tax fraud and misrepresentation of asset values. The Manhattan District Attorney's office has been particularly active, pursuing a criminal investigation that seeks to determine whether Trump and his company engaged in illegal activities concerning tax obligations and business transactions. This ongoing inquiry raises questions not only about Trump's business acumen but also about the ethical standards expected of a former president.

Another significant area of legal contention revolves around the aftermath of the 2020 presidential election. Trump has continuously made unfounded claims regarding widespread voter fraud, leading to multiple lawsuits aimed at overturning election results. Several of these legal battles have been dismissed in court, yet they have fueled a broader discourse on election integrity and voter rights. The implications of these actions extend beyond Trump's personal legal risks, as they contribute to a polarization within American politics, influencing the beliefs and behaviors of his supporters and the Republican Party as a whole.

Additionally, Trump faces civil litigation related to his actions during the January 6 insurrection at the U.S. Capitol. Various lawsuits from lawmakers and law enforcement officials claim that Trump's rhetoric incited violence and disrupted the democratic process. These cases highlight the intersection of political speech and legal accountability, raising important questions about the limits of free expression for public figures. The outcomes of these lawsuits could set precedents for accountability in political discourse and influence how future leaders communicate with their constituents.

While Trump's legal challenges are multifaceted, they also serve to reinforce the loyalty of his base. Many of his supporters view these investigations as politically motivated attacks, further solidifying their allegiance. This dynamic underscores the role that Trump's narrative of victimhood plays in modern politics, allowing him to maintain relevance and influence within the Republican Party. As these legal issues unfold, they will not only shape Trump's future but also continue to impact the broader political landscape, reflecting the ongoing debates about governance, accountability, and the rule of law in America.

Chapter 8: The Role of Trump's Base in Modern Politics

Demographics of Trump's Supporters

The demographics of Donald Trump's supporters reveal a complex tapestry of American society that played a significant role in shaping his presidency and the political landscape during and after his time in office. Understanding these demographics provides insight into the motivations and concerns that drive his base. Research indicates that his support transcended traditional political boundaries, with considerable backing from various age groups, educational backgrounds, and geographic regions. However, certain patterns emerged, particularly among white working-class voters, rural populations, and individuals with specific socioeconomic characteristics.

One notable demographic group that strongly supported Trump consists of white voters, particularly those without a college degree. This segment often felt economically marginalized and disconnected from the political elite. Many of these individuals expressed frustrations over job losses in manufacturing and a perceived lack of attention from policymakers regarding their struggles. Trump's messaging, which emphasized economic nationalism and a commitment to bringing back jobs, resonated deeply with this group, leading to a loyal voter base that viewed him as a champion of their interests.

Geographically, Trump's support was notably stronger in rural and suburban areas compared to urban centers. While urban populations tended to lean more Democratic, many rural areas experienced economic stagnation, which made Trump's promises of revitalization and infrastructure investment appealing. Additionally, his focus on issues like immigration and crime struck a chord with voters in these regions, where concerns about safety and cultural change were prevalent.

This geographical divide not only influenced voting patterns but also highlighted the broader cultural and ideological rifts in American society.

Another key demographic aspect was the significant support Trump garnered from older voters, particularly those aged 65 and older. This group often prioritized issues like healthcare and social security, and many believed that Trump would protect these programs. His strong stance against perceived threats from immigration and international trade also found favor among older voters, who feared that such changes could negatively impact their quality of life. This demographic's engagement in the electoral process underscored the importance of addressing their specific concerns during Trump's campaign and presidency.

Finally, Trump's base also included a considerable number of evangelical Christians and socially conservative voters. For many in this group, issues related to religious freedom, abortion, and family values were paramount. Trump's alignment with conservative policies, coupled with his appointment of conservative judges, solidified their support. This coalition of religious voters not only contributed to his electoral success but also played a significant role in shaping policy decisions during his administration. Ultimately, the diverse demographics of Trump's supporters illustrate the multifaceted nature of his political base and its lasting impact on American politics.

Influence on Elections and Policy

The influence of Donald J. Trump on elections and policy has been profound and multifaceted, reshaping the political landscape in the United States. His presidency marked a significant departure from traditional political norms, characterized by a populist approach that appealed directly to the concerns and aspirations of his base. This strategy not only energized a segment of the electorate that felt marginalized but also mobilized them to participate actively in the democratic process. The impact of Trump's rhetoric and policies was evident in the 2016 presidential election and continued to resonate in the 2020 election, indicating a shift in voter dynamics that could have lasting implications for American politics.

Trump's economic policies, particularly the Tax Cuts and Jobs Act of 2017, exemplify how his administration sought to influence both policy and electoral outcomes. By promising economic growth through tax reductions and deregulation, Trump aimed to appeal to business owners and middle-class voters. These policies were framed as a means to stimulate the economy, create jobs, and increase disposable income, thereby garnering support among various demographics. The tangible effects of these policies were a central theme in his campaign strategy, as he attempted to convince voters of their effectiveness and to position himself as a champion of the American worker.

Social media emerged as a critical tool for Trump's campaign and presidency, enabling him to communicate directly with the public. His mastery of platforms like Twitter allowed him to bypass traditional media filters, shaping narratives and driving political discourse on his own terms. This direct line of communication not only solidified his connection with supporters but also played a significant role in influencing public opinion and voter behavior. The ability to mobilize his base through social media proved to be a double-edged sword, fostering both loyalty and division, and highlighting the evolving nature of political communication in the digital age.

In the realm of foreign relations, Trump's approach marked a departure from established diplomatic practices, as he prioritized "America First" in his policies. This strategy influenced not only international relations but also domestic political discourse, as it prompted debates about nationalism, globalism, and their implications for U.S. interests. His relationships with leaders such as Vladimir Putin and Kim Jong-un, coupled with a contentious stance on NATO and trade agreements, shifted the focus of American foreign policy and challenged traditional alliances. This approach resonated with his base, which often expressed skepticism towards multilateral institutions and favored a more unilateral approach to international issues.

Finally, the legal challenges and investigations faced by Trump during and after his presidency have underscored the contentious nature of his influence on American politics. These challenges have sparked significant debate regarding accountability, the rule of law, and the role of the presidency in a democratic society. As voters grappled with these issues, Trump's supporters remained steadfast, often viewing the investigations as politically motivated attacks. This dynamic has not only shaped perceptions of Trump but has also highlighted the polarized nature of contemporary American politics, where loyalty to a figure can supersede traditional party affiliations and ideals. The interplay of these factors continues to define the landscape in which elections are contested and policies are formulated, leaving a lasting imprint on the American political system.

The Persistence of Populism

The persistence of populism in contemporary politics can be traced through a series of historical and cultural currents that have shaped the American political landscape. Populism, characterized by its appeal to the common people against the elite, found a renewed voice during Donald Trump's presidency. His rhetoric, often framed in stark terms of "us versus them," resonated deeply with a significant segment of the population that felt marginalized by the traditional political establishment. This sentiment was not merely a reaction to Trump's personality but rather a reflection of broader socio-economic trends that had been brewing for decades, including income inequality, job displacement due to globalization, and a growing disconnection between political leaders and their constituents.

Trump's rise was facilitated by a unique confluence of factors, including his adept use of social media as a tool for communication and mobilization. In an era where traditional media outlets were increasingly viewed with skepticism, Trump harnessed platforms like Twitter to bypass the mainstream media and speak directly to his supporters. This direct line of communication allowed him to frame narratives and control the discourse around his policies and actions. His ability to rally his base through social media not only amplified his populist messages but also catalyzed a movement that thrived on a sense of grievance and urgency, further entrenching populism into the fabric of American political discourse.

Economically, Trump's administration sought to enact policies that appealed to his core supporters, particularly in regions that had experienced significant economic decline. His focus on deregulation, tax cuts, and an "America First" trade policy was designed to resonate with working-class voters who felt left behind by previous administrations. While these policies garnered mixed results in terms of economic growth and job creation, they solidified Trump's image as a champion of the ordinary American. The populist narrative surrounding these economic measures emphasized a rejection of elite interests in favor of a more nationalist approach, which many of his supporters viewed as a necessary corrective to years of perceived neglect.

Furthermore, Trump's foreign relations strategies echoed populist sentiments, prioritizing American interests in a way that often clashed with established diplomatic norms. His administration's approach to international alliances, trade agreements, and military engagements was marked by a transactional mindset that appealed to his base's desire for a more assertive and independent America. This shift not only altered the United States' standing on the global stage but also sparked debates about the implications of populism for international relations and global cooperation. The emphasis on a nationalistic agenda underlined the tension between populist ideals and the interconnected realities of a globalized world.

The legal challenges and investigations faced by Trump during and after his presidency also reflect the complexities of populism in modern politics. While these issues were often framed by opponents as evidence of corruption and misconduct, many of his supporters interpreted them as attacks on their chosen leader and, by extension, on the populist movement itself. This perception galvanized his base, fostering a sense of loyalty and determination to defend Trump's legacy against what they viewed as a politically motivated assault. The persistence of populism, therefore, is not merely a matter of political ideology but is deeply intertwined with the emotional and psychological landscapes of American voters, making it a formidable force in shaping the future of American politics.

Chapter 9: Trump's Policies on Immigration

Border Security and Enforcement

Border security and enforcement became central themes in the Trump administration's approach to immigration policy, reflecting a commitment to a more stringent and militarized stance on the U.S.-Mexico border. The administration prioritized building a physical barrier, known colloquially as "the wall," aiming to deter illegal crossings and enhance national security. This initiative was not merely a campaign promise but transformed into a focal point of legislative and executive efforts, influencing budget allocations and policy discussions in Congress. The wall symbolized Trump's broader vision of immigration reform, which included reducing the number of undocumented immigrants and changing the dynamics of legal immigration.

In conjunction with the wall, the Trump administration implemented a series of enforcement measures that targeted both undocumented immigrants and the processes by which individuals could seek asylum. This included the controversial "zero tolerance" policy, which led to family separations at the border and sparked national and international outrage. Critics argued that these measures violated human rights and undermined the United States' historical role as a haven for those fleeing persecution. However, supporters contended that such policies were necessary to restore law and order and to send a strong message regarding the consequences of illegal immigration.

The enforcement strategies also extended to heightened scrutiny of visa programs, including H-1B visas, which are often used by tech companies to employ foreign workers. The administration sought to tighten eligibility requirements and increase the vetting processes for applicants, arguing that it would protect American jobs and wages. This shift in policy affected various sectors of the economy, particularly those reliant on skilled foreign labor, and sparked debates about the balance between protecting domestic interests and maintaining the country's competitive edge in a globalized economy.

Additionally, the Trump administration's border security policies were closely intertwined with broader themes of nationalism and populism that resonated with his base. The messaging around immigration often played on fears of crime and economic displacement, reinforcing the idea that unchecked immigration posed a direct threat to American citizens. This approach galvanized support from segments of the electorate who felt that their concerns were being overlooked by previous administrations. The discourse around border security became a rallying point for Trump's supporters, solidifying a political identity rooted in the belief that strong enforcement was synonymous with patriotism.

As the Trump presidency progressed, the implications of these border security and enforcement policies extended beyond immediate enforcement actions. They influenced the political landscape and shaped the discourse around immigration for future administrations. The legacy of these policies is a complex one, as they not only affected those seeking entry into the United States but also contributed to a polarized national debate on immigration and national identity. The ramifications of Trump's border security initiatives continue to be felt, marking a significant chapter in the ongoing narrative of American immigration policy.

Changes to Immigration Law

Changes to immigration law during President Donald J. Trump's administration marked one of the most contentious chapters in modern American politics. The president's approach fundamentally altered long-standing immigration policies, emphasizing a shift towards stricter enforcement and a more restrictive immigration framework. Among the most notable changes was the introduction of the "zero tolerance" policy, which led to the separation of families at the U.S.-Mexico border. This policy drew widespread condemnation and sparked intense national debate, highlighting the moral and ethical dilemmas surrounding immigration enforcement.

In addition to family separation, the Trump administration implemented a series of executive orders and policy changes aimed at curtailing both legal and illegal immigration. The travel ban, originally targeting several predominantly Muslim countries, exemplified Trump's hardline stance and was met with legal challenges that reached the Supreme Court. The administration also sought to eliminate the Deferred Action for Childhood Arrivals (DACA) program, which provided protections for undocumented immigrants brought to the U.S. as children. These efforts underscored a broader narrative of prioritizing national security and American jobs over humanitarian concerns.

The economic implications of these immigration law changes were significant. While Trump argued that reducing immigration would benefit American workers by lowering unemployment and increasing wages, critics contended that such policies could harm industries reliant on immigrant labor, particularly agriculture and hospitality. The administration's focus on merit-based immigration and the reduction of refugee admissions reflected a shift in how the U.S. viewed its role in global migration, with potential long-term effects on the labor market and economic growth.

Trump's immigration policies also had a profound impact on social media discourse, as individuals and organizations mobilized to either support or oppose these changes. The administration's use of platforms like Twitter allowed Trump to communicate directly with his base, framing immigration as a key issue in his political narrative. This direct engagement not only galvanized support among his followers but also polarized public opinion, leading to protests and rallies that became emblematic of the broader cultural divides within the country.

Ultimately, the changes to immigration law during Trump's presidency have left a lasting legacy that continues to shape American politics. The controversies surrounding these policies have prompted ongoing discussions about the future of immigration in the U.S., including debates over border security, the treatment of asylum seekers, and the balance between national interests and humanitarian obligations. As America navigates the complexities of immigration in a globalized world, the impact of Trump's policies will likely be a reference point for future administrations and a focal point in the evolving landscape of U.S. immigration law.

DACA and Refugee Policies

DACA, or Deferred Action for Childhood Arrivals, was a significant policy initiative implemented during the Obama administration, designed to provide temporary relief from deportation for undocumented immigrants who arrived in the United States as children. This program became a focal point of controversy during Donald Trump's presidency. While Trump initially indicated a willingness to end DACA, the legal and political ramifications of such a move created a complex landscape. The program's fate often hinged on court decisions, including a pivotal Supreme Court ruling in 2020 that blocked Trump's attempt to rescind DACA, illustrating the contentious intersection of executive power and immigration policy.

Under Trump's administration, immigration policy underwent a dramatic shift, characterized by a hardline approach that prioritized border security and enforcement over pathways to citizenship or relief for undocumented individuals. This pivot had profound implications not only for DACA recipients but also for broader immigrant populations. Policies such as family separation at the border, increased deportations, and the travel ban targeting several predominantly Muslim countries reflected a stark departure from previous administrations' more inclusive immigration strategies. These moves galvanized both supporters and opponents of Trump, shaping national discourse on immigration and human rights.

The refugee policies enacted during Trump's presidency further underscored this shift. The administration significantly reduced the cap on refugee admissions, citing national security concerns and the need to prioritize American jobs. This reduction was met with widespread criticism from humanitarian organizations and advocates for immigrant rights, who argued that the U.S. had a moral obligation to provide sanctuary to those fleeing persecution and violence. The impact of these policies extended beyond the immediate refugee population; they influenced international perceptions of the U.S. commitment to human rights and the global refugee crisis.

The role of social media during this period cannot be overlooked. Trump's administration utilized platforms like Twitter to communicate directly with his base, often bypassing traditional media channels. This strategy allowed him to frame the narrative around immigration policies, portraying them as essential for national security and economic prosperity. Supporters often rallied behind his rhetoric, viewing his hardline stance as a necessary measure to protect American interests, while opponents used social media to mobilize protests and advocate for immigrant rights, highlighting the divisive nature of the discourse.

Ultimately, the intersection of DACA and Trump's refugee policies reflects broader themes of his presidency: a prioritization of national sovereignty and security, a reshaping of the political landscape, and a mobilization of both supporters and critics. As the nation continues to grapple with the implications of these policies, the legacy of Trump's approach to immigration will likely influence American politics and societal attitudes for years to come. The challenges faced by DACA recipients and refugees serve as a testament to the enduring complexities of immigration policy in a rapidly changing political environment.

Chapter 10: Trump's Environmental and Energy Policies

Deregulation Efforts

Deregulation efforts during the Trump administration marked a significant shift in the federal government's approach to regulation and oversight across various sectors of the economy. The administration prioritized reducing the number of regulations, believing that excessive regulation stifled economic growth and innovation. This philosophy was rooted in the idea that a less intrusive government would allow businesses to thrive, create jobs, and ultimately benefit consumers through lower prices and increased choices. As part of this initiative, Trump often invoked the concept of "two out, one in," promising to eliminate two regulations for every new one introduced.

One of the most notable areas affected by deregulation was the energy sector. The Trump administration rolled back numerous environmental regulations that had been put in place during previous administrations, particularly those aimed at combating climate change. The repeal of the Clean Power Plan and the easing of restrictions on fossil fuel extraction were emblematic of this approach. Supporters argued that these changes would boost domestic energy production and lower energy costs, while critics contended that they would have long-term detrimental effects on the environment and public health.

In addition to energy, deregulation efforts extended to various industries, including finance, healthcare, and telecommunications. The administration repealed portions of the Dodd-Frank Act, which had implemented strict regulations on financial institutions following the 2008 financial crisis. Proponents of this move argued that it would encourage lending and investment, while opponents raised concerns about the potential for increased risks to the financial system. Similarly, deregulation in healthcare aimed to reduce costs and expand access, though the effectiveness of these measures remains a topic of debate.

Trump's approach to deregulation was not without controversy. Critics often highlighted the potential consequences of rolling back regulations that safeguard public welfare and the environment. Investigative reports and studies frequently pointed to the risks associated with deregulated industries, suggesting that the absence of oversight could lead to crises similar to those experienced in the past. The administration's emphasis on economic growth sometimes clashed with calls for responsible regulation, creating a polarized discussion around the balance between freedom and safety.

The impact of these deregulation efforts continues to resonate in the political landscape, shaping debates on economic policy and environmental responsibility. As the Biden administration takes a different approach, the legacy of Trump's deregulation initiatives serves as a reminder of the ongoing tensions between economic growth and regulatory oversight. The dialogue surrounding these policies illustrates the complexities of governance in a rapidly changing world, where the consequences of deregulation can have far-reaching implications for society as a whole.

Energy Independence Initiatives

Energy independence initiatives became a hallmark of the Trump administration, reflecting a commitment to reducing American reliance on foreign oil and enhancing national security. The administration's approach was multi-faceted, focusing on deregulation, the promotion of domestic energy production, and the expansion of fossil fuel resources. By rolling back numerous environmental regulations, the Trump administration aimed to stimulate the energy sector, particularly oil and gas, ultimately positioning the United States as a net energy exporter for the first time in decades.

One of the key strategies employed was the approval of major energy projects, most notably the Keystone XL and Dakota Access pipelines. These projects were marketed as essential for job creation and energy security, appealing to both the energy sector and Trump's base, which favored economic growth through infrastructure development. The administration argued that such initiatives would bolster the economy while reducing energy prices for consumers, highlighting the potential for increased employment in related industries.

In addition to fossil fuels, the Trump administration also made significant investments in nuclear energy and sought to promote coal as a viable energy source, despite its environmental implications. The focus on traditional energy sources was framed as a means of maintaining American energy dominance, which resonated with a segment of the population that viewed renewable energy initiatives as a threat to job security. This dual approach aimed to balance the needs of energy independence with economic growth, even as it faced criticism from environmental advocates and some sectors of the public.

Trade policies also played a role in Trump's energy independence initiatives, particularly in relation to oil imports. The imposition of tariffs on foreign steel and aluminum was intended to protect domestic production and reduce reliance on imports. This strategy extended to energy imports, as the administration sought to renegotiate trade agreements to prioritize American energy products. By leveraging trade policy, Trump aimed to create a more favorable landscape for U.S. energy producers, asserting that energy independence was not only an economic necessity but a strategic imperative.

The social media landscape also influenced the narrative surrounding energy independence. Through platforms like Twitter, Trump effectively communicated his administration's energy policies, often framing them in a way that resonated with his supporters. This direct communication strategy allowed him to bypass traditional media channels, fostering a narrative of energy independence that aligned with his broader political agenda. As a result, energy independence initiatives became a significant component of Trump's legacy, influencing both domestic policy and international relations in the context of global energy dynamics.

Climate Change Stance

Climate change has been a polarizing issue in American politics, and President Donald J. Trump's stance on this topic has drawn significant attention and criticism. Throughout his presidency, Trump often expressed skepticism about the scientific consensus surrounding climate change. He questioned the severity and the anthropogenic causes of global warming, positioning himself against a backdrop of economic priorities that emphasized job creation and energy independence. This skepticism resonated with a segment of the American population that prioritized economic growth over environmental regulation, reinforcing the divide in how climate issues are perceived across different political affiliations.

Trump's administration made several key policy decisions that reflected his climate change stance, most notably the withdrawal from the Paris Agreement in 2017. This international accord aimed to unify global efforts to combat climate change and limit global warming to well below two degrees Celsius. Trump's withdrawal was framed as a move to protect American jobs and industries, particularly coal and manufacturing sectors, which he argued were being unfairly burdened by international commitments. This decision was met with widespread criticism from environmentalists, scientists, and many political leaders who viewed it as a step backward in the fight against climate change.

The impact of Trump's environmental policies extended beyond international agreements. His administration rolled back numerous regulations aimed at reducing greenhouse gas emissions, including the Clean Power Plan and various vehicle emissions standards. Supporters of these rollbacks argued that they would stimulate economic growth and reduce burdensome regulations on businesses. However, critics contended that these actions would lead to increased pollution and accelerate the climate crisis, undermining efforts to transition to renewable energy sources and sustainable practices.

Trump's rhetoric on climate change also played a significant role in shaping public discourse. His frequent use of social media allowed him to bypass traditional media channels, directly communicating with his base. This approach not only solidified his support among those skeptical of climate change but also marginalized scientific voices advocating for urgent action. The framing of climate change as a hoax or an exaggerated threat found traction among certain audiences, creating a narrative that complicated bipartisan efforts to address environmental issues.

As we reflect on Trump's legacy, his climate change stance will likely be a critical component of historical analysis. The prioritization of economic interests over environmental protection during his presidency has sparked ongoing debates about the long-term implications for American politics and global climate initiatives. With the increasing urgency of climate-related challenges, examining Trump's approach offers valuable insights into the intersection of political ideology, economic policy, and environmental responsibility, shaping the discourse for future leaders and policymakers in addressing one of the most pressing issues of our time.

Chapter 11: Media Coverage of Trump: Analysis and Critique

The Relationship Between Trump and the Media

The relationship between Donald Trump and the media has been one of the most scrutinized aspects of his presidency, marked by both conflict and collaboration. From the outset of his campaign, Trump established a contentious dynamic with traditional media outlets, often labeling them as "fake news" whenever coverage did not align with his narratives. This adversarial stance not only galvanized his base but also shifted the way news was produced and consumed in the digital age. Trump's frequent use of social media, particularly Twitter, allowed him to communicate directly with the public, bypassing traditional media filters and reshaping the landscape of political discourse.

During his presidency, Trump's interactions with the media became a focal point of his administration. Press briefings often turned into confrontational exchanges, with Trump challenging reporters on their questions and framing of issues. This combative approach not only generated headlines but also contributed to a growing distrust of the media among certain segments of the population. Many of Trump's supporters viewed his criticisms as a defense against what they perceived as biased reporting, which further entrenched divisions within American society regarding what constitutes credible news.

The impact of Trump's media strategy extended beyond direct confrontations. His adeptness at utilizing social media platforms transformed the way political messages were disseminated. Trump's tweets often set the agenda for news coverage, forcing traditional outlets to react to his statements rather than the other way around. This shift has raised questions about the role of the media in democracy, as the speed and volume of information can sometimes overshadow critical analysis and fact-checking. As a result, the media landscape became increasingly polarized, with outlets aligning themselves along political lines, catering to either pro Trump or anti-Trump sentiments.

Trump's presidency also highlighted the evolving role of the media in the age of misinformation. The proliferation of alternative news sources and social media platforms has created an environment where misinformation can spread rapidly, complicating the media's ability to provide accurate reporting. This landscape posed significant challenges for journalists who sought to maintain integrity while navigating the complexities of public perception. The relationship between Trump and the media thus became emblematic of broader societal issues concerning trust, accountability, and the role of journalism in shaping public opinion.

As Trump left office, the legacy of his relationship with the media continued to resonate in American politics. The tension between political figures and the press remains a critical topic of discussion, with implications for future administrations. The ways in which Trump engaged with the media not only influenced his presidency but also set a precedent for how politicians might interact with journalists and the public in an era increasingly defined by digital communication and polarized narratives. Understanding this relationship is essential for analyzing Trump's impact on American politics and the ongoing evolution of media in the political landscape.

Coverage Bias and Its Effects

Coverage bias refers to the systematic favoritism in the way certain news stories are reported, influencing public perception and understanding of political figures and events. In the context of Donald Trump's presidency, coverage bias has played a significant role in shaping the narrative surrounding his administration. Media outlets, guided by their editorial slants, often emphasize specific aspects of Trump's policies and actions, at times neglecting others that may offer a more balanced view. This skewed reporting can contribute to a polarized political landscape, where supporters and opponents perceive fundamentally different realities based on the information they consume.

One of the most notable effects of coverage bias during Trump's presidency has been the amplification of controversies and scandals. Media focus on Trump's legal challenges, investigations, and statements often overshadowed his administration's accomplishments in areas such as economic policy and foreign relations. For instance, the robust economic growth and low unemployment rates that characterized the pre-pandemic period received comparatively less attention than the controversies surrounding his tweets or interactions with foreign leaders. This selective coverage can foster a narrative where Trump's presidency is viewed predominantly through the lens of conflict rather than achievement, thereby influencing public opinion and voter behavior.

Moreover, the rise of social media has intensified the effects of coverage bias. Platforms like Twitter and Facebook have allowed Trump to communicate directly with his base, circumventing traditional media filters. However, this direct communication has also led to an environment where misinformation can spread rapidly, further complicating public understanding of his policies and actions. The ability of users to curate their media consumption means that individuals often reinforce their existing beliefs by engaging primarily with sources that align with their views, creating echo chambers that amplify the effects of biased coverage.

Trump's foreign relations strategies, particularly his approach to contentious issues such as trade and international alliances, have also been subject to coverage bias. While some media outlets have critiqued his unorthodox methods and the potential risks associated with them, others have highlighted the successes in renegotiating trade deals or engaging in diplomacy with North Korea. The disparity in coverage can lead to divergent interpretations of these strategies, affecting both domestic and international perceptions of the United States' role on the global stage.

Ultimately, coverage bias not only impacts the public's perception of Trump but also shapes the political landscape and voter engagement. As Trump's base continues to mobilize around issues such as immigration and economic policies, the narratives constructed by media coverage will likely play a crucial role in influencing electoral outcomes. A more nuanced understanding of coverage bias is essential for citizens seeking to navigate the complexities of modern politics and for recognizing the importance of diverse media representations in fostering informed public discourse.

The Role of Alternative Media

The emergence of alternative media has significantly influenced the political landscape in the United States, particularly during the Trump presidency. During this period, traditional media faced increasing competition from platforms that provided alternative narratives, often appealing to audiences who felt marginalized or misrepresented by mainstream outlets. Alternative media, encompassing a range of independent news websites, social media platforms, and podcasts, offered a space where supporters of Donald Trump could access information that resonated with their beliefs and values. This shift not only altered how news was consumed but also how political discourse was shaped, as these platforms often prioritized sensationalism and confirmation bias.

One of the defining characteristics of alternative media during Trump's presidency was its ability to mobilize and energize his base. These platforms often presented a perspective that aligned with Trump's own rhetoric, framing issues such as immigration, economic policies, and foreign relations in ways that validated the concerns of his supporters. The narratives propagated through alternative media outlets frequently dismissed mainstream criticisms of Trump's policies, portraying them as biased or part of a larger "deep state" conspiracy. This environment fostered a sense of community among Trump supporters, reinforcing their loyalty and engagement in the political process.

Moreover, alternative media played a crucial role in shaping public perception of Trump's legal challenges and investigations. While traditional media focused on the implications of legal actions and potential consequences, alternative outlets often downplayed these issues or portrayed them as politically motivated attacks against Trump. This created a dichotomy in public opinion, where supporters were more likely to perceive legal challenges as efforts to undermine a presidency that they believed was fighting for their interests. The narratives constructed by alternative media thus contributed to a broader polarization in American politics, as supporters and opponents of Trump increasingly inhabited separate informational universes.

The rise of alternative media also had significant implications for Trump's foreign relations strategies. Coverage of international events and diplomatic relations often differed markedly between traditional and alternative media. For example, Trump's unconventional diplomacy, characterized by personal meetings with foreign leaders and a focus on America First policies, was portrayed in a more favorable light by alternative media. These platforms emphasized successes and downplayed failures, creating an image of a president who was reshaping American foreign policy in a way that benefitted ordinary citizens. This framing not only solidified Trump's standing among his base but also contributed to a sense of nationalistic pride.

Finally, the influence of alternative media has left a lasting impact on Trump's legacy and historical perspectives. As the digital landscape continues to evolve, the narratives constructed by alternative media are likely to shape how future generations perceive Trump's presidency. This phenomenon raises important questions about the role of media in democracy and the responsibilities of both traditional and alternative outlets to provide balanced and accurate information. The interplay between alternative media and Trump's presidency illustrates the complexities of modern political communication, emphasizing the need for critical media literacy in an era where information is abundant but often polarized.

Chapter 12: Trump's Legacy and Historical Perspectives

Immediate Impacts on American Society

The immediate impacts of Donald Trump's presidency on American society were profound and multifaceted, touching various aspects of daily life, politics, and the economy. One of the most significant changes was the polarization of the political landscape. Trump's ascendance to the presidency in 2016 amplified existing divisions within the electorate, as his rhetoric often appealed to a base that felt marginalized by traditional political discourse. This resulted in a heightened sense of partisanship, with supporters and detractors increasingly viewing each other through a lens of animosity rather than dialogue. The social fabric of the nation became more frayed, leading to an environment where compromise became increasingly elusive.

Trump's economic policies, including tax cuts and deregulation, presented immediate changes to American households and businesses. The Tax Cuts and Jobs Act of 2017 aimed to stimulate economic growth by lowering corporate tax rates and providing tax relief to individuals. Supporters argued that these measures would lead to job creation and increased wages, while critics contended that the benefits disproportionately favored the wealthy. As a result, the immediate impacts on the economy were mixed, with some sectors experiencing growth and others facing challenges. The economy's overall performance during Trump's tenure, particularly before the COVID-19 pandemic, reflected a period of low unemployment and rising stock markets.

Social media emerged as a powerful tool during Trump's presidency, fundamentally altering the way political communication occurred. Trump's adept use of platforms like Twitter allowed him to bypass traditional media channels and speak directly to the public. This approach not only enabled him to rally his base but also fostered a culture of instant reactions and misinformation. The immediacy of social media amplified the impact of Trump's statements, often leading to viral news cycles that shaped public perception. This shift in communication dynamics also raised questions about accountability and the role of technology in political discourse, as the line between fact and opinion became increasingly blurred.

In terms of foreign relations, Trump's presidency marked a departure from established diplomatic norms. His approach often favored personal relationships with world leaders over traditional multilateralism, leading to significant shifts in alliances and global policies. The immediate impact was felt in the United States' relationships with key allies and adversaries alike, as Trump's policies towards NATO, China, and North Korea evoked both support and criticism. This realignment prompted discussions on the effectiveness of traditional diplomatic approaches and raised concerns about America's role on the global stage.

Lastly, Trump's presidency brought legal challenges that reverberated throughout American society. Ongoing investigations into his business practices, allegations of collusion with foreign powers, and impeachment proceedings introduced an era of political drama that captivated the nation. These legal issues not only dominated headlines but also contributed to the growing skepticism towards established institutions. As citizens grappled with the implications of these challenges, the immediate impact was a heightened awareness of the intersection between politics and the law, raising critical questions about governance, accountability, and the future of American democracy.

Long-Term Historical Viewpoints

The presidency of Donald J. Trump represents a significant moment in American history, evoking a wide spectrum of responses across political, economic, and social landscapes. To understand the long-term implications of Trump's presidency, it is essential to examine it through the lens of historical continuity and change. His administration's policies and actions have not only shaped contemporary politics but also reflect deeper historical trends, particularly regarding populism, partisanship, and the evolving role of media in political discourse. Analyzing these trends provides insight into how Trump's presidency may be viewed in future historical narratives.

One of the most notable aspects of Trump's presidency is its alignment with a broader historical trend of populism in American politics. Populist leaders have emerged at various points in U.S. history, often responding to economic grievances and perceived elitism in governance. Trump's rise can be connected to these historical cycles, where discontent with the status quo has propelled unconventional candidates into power. His ability to resonate with a disenchanted voter base highlights a recurring theme in American politics: the struggle between established political norms and the demand for change from below. This dynamic has implications for how future historians may interpret the legitimacy and impact of his presidency.

Economically, Trump's administration marked a departure from previous policies, particularly in its approach to taxation and regulation. The Tax Cuts and Jobs Act of 2017, which aimed to stimulate economic growth through significant tax reductions, reflects a historical inclination towards supply-side economics. However, the long-term effects of these policies, including income inequality and federal deficit concerns, will be subjects of scrutiny for historians assessing Trump's economic legacy. The decisions made during this period will likely influence economic discussions for decades, as they challenge the traditional paradigms of fiscal responsibility and economic equity.

Trump's foreign relations strategies, characterized by an "America First" philosophy, also warrant a historical examination. This approach has roots in earlier American isolationist trends but has evolved to encompass a more aggressive stance towards international alliances and trade agreements. The withdrawal from international accords and the re-evaluation of longstanding partnerships signal a shift that may redefine America's position on the global stage. Historians will need to consider how these decisions resonate with past foreign policy doctrines and what they mean for future international relations, particularly in an increasingly multipolar world.

As we look back on Trump's presidency through these long-term historical viewpoints, it is essential to consider the role of social media as both a tool and a battleground for political discourse. Trump's unique use of platforms like Twitter transformed the relationship between politicians and the public, breaking down traditional barriers of communication. This phenomenon reflects a significant historical shift in how political narratives are constructed and disseminated. Future analyses will likely delve into the implications of this transformation for democracy, civic engagement, and the very nature of political authority. Ultimately, Trump's presidency, viewed through a historical lens, offers rich material for understanding the interplay of political power, public sentiment, and the media in shaping American history.

Assessing the Future of Trumpism

Assessing the future of Trumpism involves understanding its foundational elements and the evolving political landscape. Trumpism represents a complex blend of populist sentiment, nationalist rhetoric, and a distinct approach to governance that emerged during Donald J. Trump's presidency. This ideology has reshaped the Republican Party and American politics at large, creating a polarizing yet impactful legacy. Key to assessing its future is recognizing how these elements resonate with both Trump's base and the broader electorate, as well as the potential for adaptation or transformation in response to changing societal dynamics.

One significant aspect of Trumpism is its economic policies, which prioritized deregulation, tax cuts, and an "America First" trade approach. These policies garnered support from various demographics, particularly working-class voters who felt overlooked by traditional political elites. As the economy evolves and new challenges arise, such as inflation and global supply chain disruptions, the effectiveness and popularity of these economic strategies will be tested. Future iterations of Trumpism may need to address these economic realities while maintaining the core principles that resonate with its supporters.

Social media has played a pivotal role in amplifying Trumpism, allowing for direct communication between Trump and his followers, bypassing traditional media channels. The rise of platforms like Twitter and Facebook facilitated a unique form of engagement that reshaped political discourse. Looking ahead, the impact of social media on Trumpism remains critical, especially as platforms evolve and face scrutiny over misinformation and content regulation. The ability of Trump and his supporters to adapt their messaging and strategies in this changing digital landscape will significantly influence the movement's longevity and relevance.

Foreign relations strategies under Trump's administration, characterized by an unpredictable and often confrontational stance, have left a lasting imprint on international diplomacy. The embrace of unilateralism and skepticism towards multilateral agreements reshaped alliances and global perceptions of the United States. As future leaders navigate a multipolar world, the principles of Trumpism may inform a new approach to foreign policy that prioritizes national sovereignty and economic interests. However, this approach will need to balance isolationist tendencies with the realities of global interdependence.

Legal challenges and investigations surrounding Trump have also played a crucial role in the narrative of Trumpism. As these issues unfold, they create a backdrop that may either galvanize his base or alienate moderate supporters. The outcome of these legal battles will likely influence perceptions of Trumpism and its viability in the future. Furthermore, the role of Trump's base in modern politics is essential to understanding the movement's trajectory. Their loyalty and activism could either sustain or undermine the ideology, as the party navigates internal divisions and the search for a unifying figure post-Trump.

Don't miss out!

Visit the website below and you can sign up to receive emails whenever Stephen G. publishes a new book. There's no charge and no obligation.

https://books2read.com/r/B-A-VPPMC-BDIBF

BOOKS 2 READ

Connecting independent readers to independent writers.